Contents

S0-BER-528

More Great Books in the Warman's Field Guide Series

Warman's® Bean Plush Field Guide
Disney® Collectibles Field Guide
Pepsi Field Guide
U.S. Coins & Currency Field Guide, 2nd Edition
Vintage Guitars Field Guide
Watches Field Guide
Dolls Field Guide
Field Guide to Precious Moments Collectibles
Jewelry Field Guide
Kitschy Kitchen Collectibles Field Guide
Zippo Lighters Field Guide
Fishing Lures Field Guide, 2nd Edition
Coca-Cola Field Guide
Tools Field Guide
Star Wars Field Guide
Action Figures Field Guide
G.I. Joe Field Guide
Transformers Field Guide
Barbie Doll Field Guide
Hot Wheels Field Guide
Matchbox Field Guide

Warman's
Lunch Boxes
FIELD GUIDE

Joe Soucy

All photos by Paul Brissman

Values and Identification

©2008 Krause Publications
Published by

kp krause publications
An Imprint of F+W Publications

700 East State Street • Iola, WI 54990-0001
715-445-2214 • 888-457-2873
www.krausebooks.com

Our toll-free number to place an order or obtain a free catalog is (800) 258-0929.

Library of Congress Control Number: 2008928405
ISBN 13-digit: 978-0-89689-726-7
ISBN 10-digit: 0-89689-726-5

Designed by Kay Sanders
Edited by Joe Kertzman

Printed in China

What is a Field Guide?

Welcome to Warman's Lunch Boxes Field Guide. First, let's define a couple of important terms you'll see throughout this book. A "lunch box" is the colorful companion of generations of school kids that did more than hold lunch—its designs displayed favorite television and film characters. A "bottle" is the container for holding liquids that came in most lunch boxes. A common term for bottle is Thermos™, but that is a trademarked name much the way that facial tissues are commonly called Kleenex™.

This Field Guide is an introduction to the lunch box collecting hobby. It contains lunch boxes and Thermoses from the 1950s to the 1980s. Lunch boxes of this period were produced in steel, vinyl, and plastic. The steel boxes are the most popular among collectors and are the subject of this book. Because this Field Guide serves as an introduction to the hobby, not every steel lunch box and accompanying Thermos ever produced is presented here.

The book contains a wide variety of lunch boxes from the very first themed box (Hopalong Cassidy), to the most valuable lunch box (Superman, 1954), to more common releases like Muppet Babies and The Dukes of Hazzard. Ever wonder what the lunch box you carried to school is worth? You'll probably find it within these pages.

See the "How To Use This Book" information on page 7 for instructions to find the boxes you seek among the alphabetical listings.

A Note on Value

The author for this project is Joe Soucy of Seaside Toys. A veteran lunch box collector and dealer, Soucy is noted for his auctions of pristine-condition lunch boxes and bottles. He shared some excellent advice regarding values.

"The key word for value is always condition—finding a rare box in poor condition will reduce its value considerably. Some collectors are willing to accept a rare box in lesser condition, but you can go overboard and pay too much for a lesser condition box just to have one, so collectors must exercise good judgment."

The values presented here are only a guide to value, and ultimately the worth of a particular lunch box and bottle lies with the buyer and seller.

If you would like to contact Joe Soucy, he may be reached at the following address:

**Seaside Toys
179 Main St.
Westerly, RI 02891
Phone: 401-596-0962**

Enjoy this colorful introduction to the wonderful world of lunch boxes, and support your local area toy shows!

How To Use This Book

The lunch boxes contained in this Field Guide are presented in alphabetical order.

The text under each picture contains information about that lunch box or bottle in the following order: name of the item, the name of the company that manufactured the item, the year the item was produced, and the value in Near Mint/Mint condition for the item. Near mint is defined as a lightly used box or bottle, whereas a Mint example is totally unused, though it may have small scuff marks from shelf wear.

Trends in Today's Lunch Box Market

By Noah Fleisher

Whether you're a seasoned veteran or neophyte lunch box collector, the good news is that, in today's market with a soft economy, it's more than ever a buyer's market.

According to Joe Soucy, acknowledged expert and author of this field guide, in a market like today's, what a buyer normally sees is a premium for high-profile character boxes, while prices on lesser characters, and what he calls more common and non-character boxes go down.

"Today I see that condition is a really important factor in what people are buying, along with major character items," he said. "Something from a TV series, like the Brady Bunch or The Waltons, these boxes still have a good market value."

The "common" boxes, like plaids, floral patterns or non-character boxes, which normally might sell for anywhere between $75 and $150, are where collectors can use the current drop-off in prices to bolster their collections for when the economy, and the lunch box market, come back around.

There is a truism that applies to all levels of collecting, whether it's lunch boxes, fine art, costume jewelry or Matchbox cars.

"Good is always good," said Soucy, "and it will *always* be good. In lunch boxes, super stuff like Underdog, Rocky and Bullwinkle or Dudley Do-Right, if condition is there, the price is very substantial. Strong character items will usually hold their value."

The number of collectors that can usually go after the top-of-the-line character boxes, however, is limited. The majority of collectors who pursue their hobby part-time can't go after the 1954 Superman lunch box in near mint to mint condition. Most of them can acquire the minor character boxes or the more common boxes, especially in today's market.

Take, for instance, a box that might have brought $150 two years ago: A collector looking at that same box today on eBay, or consigned through a dealer, may well be able to pick it up for around $50. In a short time, combined with a little bit of patience, a substantial collection can be put together and significant value realized as long as he or she can wait out the soft market.

"In terms of the minor boxes," Soucy said, "there's usually a very slight fluctuation in those values; they may waffle a little bit, but they won't nosedive."

There's also a distinct possibility of finding a rare box for very little, which isn't so much a trend as it is dumb luck. As Soucy says, it is always possible. However he points to a Rocky and Bullwinkle prototype lunch box that appeared on eBay in May of 2008.

"It's in the top 10 of the rarest boxes made," he said. "To date only five of this same box have surfaced."

It turned out that the seller wasn't aware of what he or she had, and had listed it with the "Buy It Now" feature for a mere $185. A lucky collector, who also didn't necessarily know what he or she was looking at, bought it at the arranged price. It turns out, for the $185 investment, the collector walked away with a $3,000 box.

That, however, is the exception to the rule. For the most part, the current market supports the low-end boxes and prices, and buyers would be smart to focus on the lower end of the market, where boxes that are toward the bottom of their price fluctuation can be had for a virtual song. It's in this way that solid collections are put together, and capital stocked to make the big deals when they come along.

So You Want to Collect Lunch Boxes?

By Noah Fleisher

The human urge to collect is primal. There are a myriad of reasons why a person decides to collect this or that; those reasons number as many as people on the planet. When it comes to the antiques and collectibles market, though, there is usually one driving factor that pushes people into it: nostalgia.

There is little that is stronger in people who were kids in the 1950s, '60s and '70s than the sense of nostalgia for those decades past. The '50s-'70s represented a time in American life that was decidedly simpler in terms of technology, television and society. It was also in these decades that lunch boxes saw their heyday.

"It's going back into your childhood," said Joe Soucy. "Lunch boxes conjure up memories in your mind. A lot of times I've seen people go after what they had when they were a kid or they go after the ones that their mother wouldn't buy them when they were a kid."

The other avenue that leads collectors to the pursuit of lunch boxes, said Soucy, is an attraction to the artwork of the boxes.

That may seem, at first, a bit comical, but the artwork on the best of lunch boxes is a true testament to the artistic styles and design philosophies of the time in which they were produced. Some can be quite striking, with bold color choices. In this way, many transcend their origins as simple lunch boxes and become a form of industrial pop art.

"If you focus on it, the art really is nice," said Soucy. "It locks in a time period of this country that's no longer there. Life was a lot simpler then."

If you are considering getting into the lunch box game these days, the ways for you to approach the hobby are numerous. There's the old school approach, which is simply getting out and beating the bushes at antique shows, yard sales, consignment shops and flea markets. It's still a viable method to build a collection, said Soucy, but not necessarily the way that the majority of people are doing it these days.

The way that most people are doing it should be fairly obvious to anyone who's bought anything online in the past decade: eBay. There you can find a wide array of boxes from the 1950s through 1985, when metal lunch boxes went out of production.

EBay is the place where much of the commerce in lunch boxes happens, the place that the high end and the low end of the market mix freely, and buyers of all stripes can see what fair market value is.

"On eBay," said Soucy, "no matter how rare or common something is, it will find its fair market value."

That doesn't mean, though, that you should or can just log on and start buying whatever lunch boxes suit your fancy.

Along with guides, such as this book and collectors like Soucy who have a vested interest in seeing the hobby flourish, you should take your time, do your research and watch how various sales pan out. The availability, like so many other areas of the market, is not what it was 10 or 15 years ago. The Internet has taken care of that. Most attics and basements have been cleaned out and very few spectacular finds are to be had for rock bottom prices.

Getting into the open market and seeing what's available on the floors of shows and shops is a good education, especially when coupled with a digital approach via eBay. In this way, even the collector with absolutely no experience can get a quick degree in lunch box collecting and start assembling their own collection within a few weeks.

On this and the next page are examples of the original boxes that Aladdin used for lunch box bottles. Above are Tom Corbett Space Cadet and Hopalong Cassidy boxes.

Here are original Annie Oakley and Zorro boxes from
Aladdin.

18 Wheeler, Aladdin, 1978, **$175.**

18 Wheeler Bottle, Aladdin, 1978, **$25.**

240 Robert, Aladdin, 1978, **$5,500.**

Did you know...
Action Jackson toys, produced by Mego, tried to rival G.I. Joe in the early 1970s. While the toys didn't fair as well as Joe, the lunch box has become a classic.

Action Jackson, Okay Industries, 1973, **$1,500.**

Action Jackson Bottle, Okay Industries, 1973, **$650.**

Adam-12, Aladdin, 1973, **$450.**

Adam-12 Bottle, Aladdin, 1973, **$100.**

Did you know...

Based on the 1970s cartoon of the same name, itself based on the live action TV show of the 1960s, the front of the box curiously features neither Gomez nor Morticia.

Addams Family, King Seeley Thermos, 1974, **$425.**

Addams Family Bottle, King Seeley Thermos, 1974, **$50.**

Did you know...

One of the earliest Universal lunch boxes, this mid-1950s model features the continental United States, pre-Hawaii and Alaska.

All American, Universal, 1954, **$525.**

All American Bottle, Universal, 1954, **$125.**

Americana, American Thermos, 1958, **$425.**

Americana Bottle, American Thermos, 1958, **$165.**

Did you know...

Annie Oakley and her brother Tagg ran for three seasons in the mid-1950s on ABC-TV, then again on weekends in the late '50s and mid-1960s. A total of 81 episodes were filmed, starring Gail Davis in the title role.

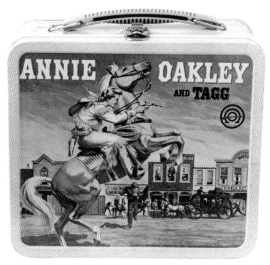

Annie Oakley, Aladdin, 1955, **$725**

Annie Oakley Bottle, Aladdin, 1955, **$175.**

Archies, The, Aladdin, 1969, **$325.**

Archies, The, Bottle, Aladdin, 1969, **$75.**

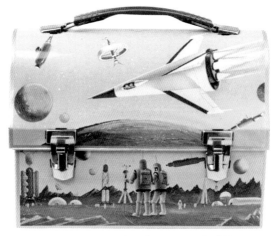

Astronaut, King Seeley Thermos, 1960, **$280.**

Astronaut Bottle, same bottle was used for Satellite box,
King Seeley Thermos, 1960, **$75.**

Astronauts, Aladdin, 1969, **$325.**

Astronauts Bottle, Aladdin, 1969, **$95.**

Did you know...

Atom Ant was part of Hanna-Barbera's first superhero duo, along with James Bond-inspired Secret Squirrel, in 1966. Along with Atom and Secret, Squiddley Diddley, The Hillbilly Bears, Precious Pupp and Winsome Witch ran for three seasons.

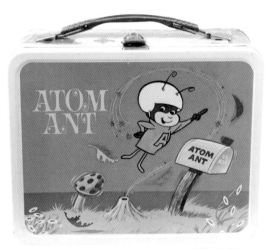

Atom Ant, King Seeley Thermos, 1966, **$360.**

Atom Ant Bottle, King Seeley Thermos, 1966, **$120.**

Auto Race, King Seeley Thermos, 1967, **$280.**

Auto Race, back of box.

Auto Race Bottle, King Seeley Thermos, 1967, **$75.**

Did you know...

Aladdin produced a whole host of bicentennial-inspired products, including this 1975 lunch box showing George Washington getting his shoes shined. One would imagine it was before going to face the redcoats, or perhaps his inauguration as President?

Back in '76, Aladdin, 1975, **$110.**

Back in '76 Bottle, Aladdin, 1975, **$40.**

Barbie & Midge, American Thermos, Canada, 1960s, **$250.**

Barbie & Midge Bottle, American Thermos,
Canada, 1960s, **$60.**

Did you know...

*Two of the most enduring of pop culture characters,
Batman and Robin graced more than their fair
share of lunch boxes and toys. This box, from 1966,
is one of the more popular boxes, bringing the hefty
sum of **$700** when it can be found.*

Batman, Aladdin, 1966, **$700.**

Batman Bottle, Aladdin, 1966, **$175.**

Batman,
back of
box.

Did you know...

Capitalizing on the mid-1960s popularity of World War II movies, TV shows, comics and toys, like G.I. Joe, King Seeley Thermos produced the Battle Kit lunch box for the boy who lived for G.I. Joe but couldn't get one of the boxes.

Battle Kit, King Seeley Thermos, 1965, **$350.**

Battle Kit Bottle, King Seeley Thermos, 1965, **$75.**

Did you know...

A popular movie and TV show, Battlestar Galactica was an effort to capitalize on the Star Wars craze. This lunch box was a must for eight- and nine-year-olds in the late-1970s, and, at **$275,** *still affordable for those boys who never quite grew up.*

Battlestar Galactica, Aladdin, 1978, **$275.**

Battlestar Galactica Bottle, Aladdin, 1978, **$45.**

Did you know...

 What is there to say about The Fab Four? Surely they embodied the greatest rock band of all time, and surely one of the greatest marketing machines of all time. This lunch box is one of the rarest and most popular in the world, as evidenced by the price.

Beatles, Aladdin, 1966, **$2,800.**

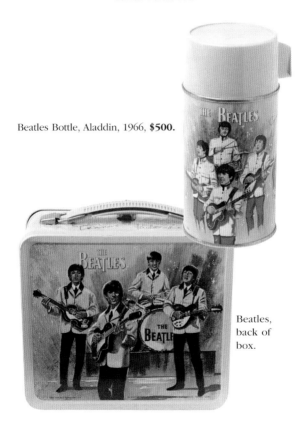

Beatles Bottle, Aladdin, 1966, **$500.**

Beatles, back of box.

Bedknobs and Broomsticks, Aladdin, 1972, **$250.**

Bedknobs and Broomsticks Bottle, Aladdin, 1972, **$65.**

Beverly Hillbillies, The, Aladdin, 1963, **$375.**

Beverly Hillbillies, The, Bottle, Aladdin, 1963, **$95.**

Bionic Woman, The, Aladdin, 1977-78, **$275.**

Bionic Woman, The, back of box for 1977 version.

Bionic Woman, The, back of box for 1978 version.

Bionic Woman, The, Bottle, Aladdin, **$50.**

Black Hole, The, Aladdin, 1979, **$95.**

Black Hole, The, Bottle, Aladdin, 1979, **$40.**

Blondie, King Seeley Thermos, 1969, **$350.**

Blondie Bottle, King Seeley Thermos, 1969, **$75.**

Boating, American Thermos, 1959, **$450.**

Boating Bottle, American Thermos, 1959, **$125.**

Did you know...

Bonanza ran for 14 years, from 1959 to 1973, and was one of the longest running TV shows in history. The adventures of the Cartwrights, always defending the Ponderosa, play out on both sides of this 1963 lunch box.

Bonanza, Aladdin, 1963, **$400.**

Bonanza Bottle, Aladdin, 1963, **$110.**

Bonanza, more common, Aladdin, 1965, **$300.**

Bonanza Bottle, Aladdin, 1965, **$75.**

Bonanza, Aladdin, 1968, **$475.**

Bonanza Bottle, Aladdin, 1968, **$120.**

Did you know...

One of stars of the Sid & Marty Kroft live action stable of the early 1970s, The Bugaloos were a multi-cultural English psychedelic rock band who buzzed around with Sparky the Firefly, played by the legendary Billy Barty.

Bugaloos, Aladdin, 1971, **$425.**

Bugaloos Bottle, Aladdin, 1971, **$75.**

NHL Bottle, also used for Boston Bruins box, Okay Industries, **$250.**

Boston Bruins, Okay Industries, 1973, **$525.**

Did you know...

A moderately priced box, due to the availability of decent examples, Bozo is still probably the most famous clown in the world, though he's been off TV since 1994. The long-lived clown started making children laugh in 1949, and is a frequent write-in name for President.

Bozo the Clown, Aladdin, 1963, **$375.**

Bozo the Clown Bottle, Aladdin, 1963, **$120**.

Brady Bunch, The, King Seeley Thermos, 1970, **$575.**

Brady Bunch Bottle, King Seeley Thermos, 1970, **$150.**

Buccaneer Dome, Aladdin, 1959, **$425.**

Buccaneer Bottle, Aladdin, 1959, **$125.**

Buck Rogers in the 25th Century, Aladdin, 1979, **$120.**

Buck Rogers in the 25th Century Bottle, Aladdin, 1979, **$35.**

Did you know...

One of the most popular and enduring cartoons from the late 1950s and 1960s, the Bullwinkle lunch box is one of the very top character boxes ever produced. When one of the rare boxes comes on the block, prices routinely soar into the **$3,000-$4,000** *range.*

Bullwinkle and Rocky, Okay Industries, 1962, **$3,500.**

Bullwinkle and Rocky Bottle, Okay Industries, 1962, **$1,500.**

Cable Car Dome, Aladdin, 1962, **$600.**

Cable Car Bottle, Aladdin, 1962, **$125.**

Campbell Kids, Okay Industries, 1975, **$285.**

Campbell Kids Bottle, rare, Okay Industries, 1975, **$150.**

Campus Queen, King Seeley Thermos, 1967, **$265.**

Campus Queen Bottle, King Seeley Thermos, 1967, **$75.**

Captain Astro, Ohio Arts, 1966, **$600.**

Carnival, Universal, 1959, **$750.**

Carnival Bottle, Universal, 1959, **$250.**

Did you know...

Hannah-Barbera's tried and true Yogi Bear formula worked well for its Cartoon Zoo as well. Characters like Hokey Wolf, Wally Gator and Ding-a-ling Lion all had human straight characters to play off of in, basically, the same plot.

Cartoon Zoo, Universal, 1963, **$600.**

Cartoon Zoo Bottle, Universal, 1963, **$125.**

Casey Jones, this is the only metal dome box Universal
ever made, Universal, 1960, **$650.**

Casey Jones Bottle, Universal, 1960, **$125.**

Did you know...

American Thermos made some great metal dome boxes, and the Central Firehouse, with its detailed artwork and waving American flag, truly captures the patriotic feeling of Cold War America in the late 1950s.

Central Firehouse or Firehouse, American Thermos, 1959, **$475.**

Central Firehouse or Firehouse Bottle,
American Thermos, 1959, **$150.**

Charlie's Angles, Aladdin, 1978, **$250.**

Charlie's Angles Bottle, Aladdin, 1978, **$50.**

Chavo, Aladdin, 1979, **$285.**

Chavo Bottle, Aladdin, 1979, **$50.**

Chitty Chitty Bang Bang, King Seeley Thermos,
1969, **$400.**

Chitty Chitty Bang Bang Bottle, King Seeley Thermos,
1969, **$75.**

Chuck Connors Cowboy in Africa, King Seeley Thermos, 1968, **$350.**

Chuck Connors Cowboy in Africa Bottle, King Seeley Thermos, 1968, **$75.**

Circus Wagon Dome, Aladdin, 1958, **$350.**

Circus Wagon Bottle, Aladdin, 1958, **$150.**

Did you know...

Produced at a time when the space race was just heating up, the Col. Ed McCauley lunch box reflected not only the nation's fascination with space exploration in the early 1960s, but also the belief in America's supremacy. Notice the space ship, which is strangely similar to the Space Shuttle, still some 20 years away.

Col. Ed McCauley, Aladdin, 1960, **$675.**

Col. Ed McCauley Bottle, Aladdin, 1960, **$125.**

Color Me Happy, Ohio Arts, 1984, **$375.**

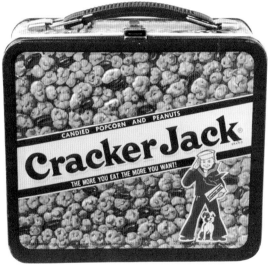

Cracker Jack, Aladdin, 1979, **$150.**

Cracker Jack Bottle, Aladdin, 1979, **$50.**

Did you know...

An officially sanctioned Walt Disney lunch box, this 1955 gem doesn't exactly reflect the family friendly profile Disney so fervently strives for these days. Davy is swinging his rifle wildly at Santa Ana's attacking troops, and engaging in a knife vs. axe battle on the back.

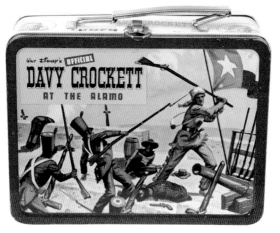

Davy Crockett at the Alamo, Adco, 1955, **$1,800.**

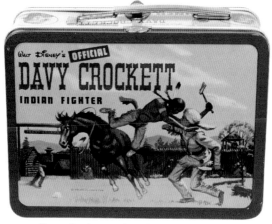

Davy Crockett at the Alamo, back of box.

Davy Crockett at the Alamo Bottle,
front, Adco, 1955, **$3,500.**

Davy Crockett, American Thermos, 1955, **$375.**

Davy Crockett Bottle, American Thermos, 1955, **$75.**

Davy Crockett King of the Wild Frontier or Davy Crockett/Kit Carson, Adco, 1955, **$350.**

Davy Crockett King of the Wild Frontier, back of box.

Davy Crockett King of the Wild Frontier, two different sidebands used.

Davy Crockett, Kruger Canada, 1955, **$900.**

Davy Crockett, back of box.

Did you know...

Though Dick Tracy had seen his heyday some 20 to 25 years before this box was produced, Dick remained one of the most enduring and popular comic, cartoon, TV and movie characters until his run ended and Chester Gould stopped drawing him in 1977.

Dick Tracy, Aladdin, 1967, **$450.**

Dick Tracy Bottle, Aladdin, 1967, **$125.**

Disco Fever, Aladdin, 1980, **$150.**

Disney on Parade, Aladdin, 1970, **$100.**

Disney on Parade Bottle, Aladdin, 1970, **$30.**

Disney School Bus, Aladdin, 1961, **$150.**

Disney School Bus Bottle, Aladdin, 1961, **$40.**

Did you know...

The Disneyland Monorail lunch box represents a time in America when Disneyland was America's biggest and favorite theme park, and the monorail was thought to be a viable mode of transportation for the future. The value of the box has held off, though not the value of monorails.

Disneyland Monorail, Aladdin, 1960, **$725.**

Disneyland Monorail Bottle, Aladdin, 1960, **$125.**

Disneyland The White Castle, Aladdin, 1957, **$650.**

Disneyland The White Castle Bottle, Aladdin, 1957, **$125.**

Dr. Dolittle, Aladdin, 1968, **$350.**

Dr. Dolittle Bottle, Aladdin, 1968, **$90.**

Did you know...

With the Cat in the Hat, Dr. Seuss revolutionized the world of children's literature. From the time of its publication in 1957, through today, more than a half-century later, the title Cat, along with Thing 1 and Thing 2, continue to engage children of all ages.

Dr. Seuss, Aladdin, 1970, **$525.**

Dr. Seuss, back of box.

Dr. Seuss Bottle, Aladdin, 1970, **$75.**

Drag Strip, Aladdin, 1975, **$200.**

Drag Strip Bottle, Aladdin, 1975, **$45.**

Did you know...

Another of the hobby's most sought-after names, Dudley Do-Right continues to inspire high prices and a boatload of nostalgia among collectors of high-profile character boxes. A box like this will never lose value and remains relatively unaffected by economic fluctuations.

Dudley Do-Right, Okay Industries, 1962, **$3,450.**

Dudley Do-Right Bottle, Okay Industries, 1962, **$1,450.**

Did you know...

*The popularity and enduring kitsch value of The
Dukes of Hazzard TV show is probably what makes
this box desirable among minor box collectors.
Boxes from 1980 rarely break* **$200,** *so The Dukes
are a notable exception.*

Dukes of Hazzard, The, Aladdin, 1980, **$225.**

Dukes of Hazzard, The, Bottle, same used for Dukes
Cousins box, Aladdin, 1980, **$50.**

Dukes of Hazzard, The, a.k.a. Dukes Cousins,
Aladdin, 1983, **$175.**

Did you know...

If Scooby Doo was a hit with a scruffy sidekick like Shaggy, then what was to stop Hannah-Barbera from applying a similar format to a super hero cartoon? Apparently nothing, and the ratings and limited popularity of the show proved that some ideas are best kept on the drawing board.

Dynomutt, King Seeley Thermos, 1977, **$150.**

E.T., Aladdin, 1982, **$125.**

E.T. Bottle, Aladdin, 1982, **$25.**

Emergency!, Aladdin, 1973, **$350.**

Emergency! Dome, Aladdin, 1977, **$400.**

Emergency! Bottle, same bottle used for both boxes,
Aladdin, **$50.**

Did you know...

The hero of a generation of young boys from the mid-1960s through the 1970s, Evel was the ultimate daredevil. He jumped busses, canyons and sharks, defying death at every turn. This lunch box is just part of a large line of toys that were a must for any little boy in 1974.

Evel Knievel, Aladdin, 1974, **$275.**

Evel Knievel Bottle, Aladdin, 1974, **$55.**

Fall Guy, The, Aladdin, 1981, **$85.**

Fall Guy, The, Bottle, Aladdin, 1981, **$30.**

Family Affair, King Seeley Thermos, 1969, **$375.**

Family Affair Bottle, King Seeley Thermos, 1969, **$90.**

Did you know...

While not particularly valuable, the Fat Albert and the Cosby Kids lunch box is one of a very few—if not the only—lunch box that features minority characters, much like the cartoon it is based upon.

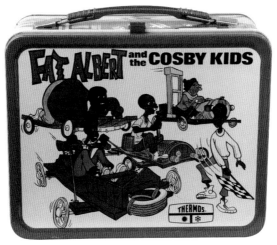

Fat Albert and the Cosby Kids, King Seeley Thermos, 1973, **$120.**

Fat Albert and the Cosby Kids Bottle, King Seeley
Thermos, 1973, **$30.**

Did you know...

Fireball XL-5 should not be confused with Planet Patrol in the states, but it's an easy thing to do. Fireball was a BBC product, but had the same marionettes, and it looks like the same props and more than likely the same plots. The box, however, is a true artistic original.

Fireball XL-5, King Seeley Thermos, 1964, **$400.**

Fireball XL-5 Bottle, the second series bottle is on the left
and the first series bottle is on the right,
King Seeley Thermos, **$85.**

Flag-O-Rama, has flags from the original United Nations on box, Universal, 1954, **$475.**

Flag-O-Rama Bottle, Universal, 1954, **$110.**

Did you know...

*With The Flintstones 1962 and '64 lunch boxes,
it's the '64 version that is worth more, both
capitalizing on the popularity of the first prime
time cartoon. Strangely, though, the art on neither
box really captures the spirit of the show itself.*

Flintstones, The, and Dino, Aladdin, 1962, **$600**.

Flintstones, The, and Dino Bottle, Aladdin, 1962, **$110.**

Flintstones, The, Aladdin, 1964, **$675.**

Flintstones, The, back of box.

Flintstones, The, Bottle, Aladdin, 1964, **$110.**

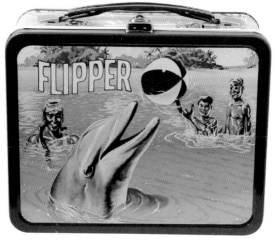

Flipper, King Seeley Thermos, 1966, **$350.**

Flipper Bottle, King Seeley Thermos, 1966, **$75.**

Did you know...

*Sally Field as The Flying Nun did well on TV,
and obviously so in marketing. While not a major
character lunch box, as you can see, she still brings
almost $500, and still makes flying look fun.*

Flying Nun, Aladdin, 1968, **$475.**

Flying Nun Bottle, Aladdin, 1968, **$95.**

Fonz, The, King Seeley Thermos, 1978, **$250.**

Fraggle Rock, King Seeley Thermos, 1984, **$110.**

Fraggle Rock Bottle, King Seeley Thermos, 1984, **$30.**

Fritos Corn Chips, King Seeley Thermos, 1975, **$300.**

Did you know...

With an early depiction of Tony the Tiger, the 1969 Frosted Flakes lunch box reflects the popularity of the character at the time. This lunch box was also a very good example of a corporate icon and logo making a successful transformation into pop culture.

Frosted Flakes a.k.a. Tony the Tiger, Aladdin, 1969, **$450.**

Frosted Flakes a.k.a. Tony the Tiger Bottle,
Aladdin, 1969, **$75.**

Funtastic World of Hanna-Barbera, The,
King Seeley Thermos, 1977, **$350.**

Funtastic World of Hanna-Barbera, The, Bottle, used for both boxes, King Seeley Thermos, **$45.**

Funtastic World of Hanna-Barbera, The,
King Seeley Thermos, 1978, **$375.**

G.I. Joe, King Seeley Thermos, 1967, **$425.**

G.I. Joe Bottle, King Seeley Thermos, 1967, **$90.**

G.I. Joe, King Seeley Thermos, 1982, **$125.**

G.I. Joe Bottle, King Seeley Thermos, 1982, **$25.**

Did you know...

A true original, a true beauty and a true piece of folk art, there's nothing about this Gene Autry lunch box that doesn't perfectly capture America in the mid-1950s. With a price like that for a "10," it's obvious that collectors think so, too.

Gene Autry, Universal, 1954, **$1,850.**

Gene Autry Bottle, Universal, 1954, **$225.**

Gentle Ben, Aladdin, 1968, **$225.**

Gentle Ben Bottle, first
version, Aladdin, 1968, **$75.**

Gentle Ben Bottle, second
version, Aladdin, **$75.**

Did you know...

Maxwell Smart, Agent 99 and a fluffy dog. Who could not like that? The super spy has always been hot, and this lunch box reflects that enduring popularity. From the fertile minds of Mel Brooks and Buck Henry, Get Smart has never lost its appeal.

Get Smart, King Seeley Thermos, 1966, **$725.**

Get Smart Bottle, King Seeley Thermos, 1966, **$95.**

Gomer Pyle, Aladdin, 1966, **$450.**

Gomer Pyle Bottle,
Aladdin, 1966, **$110.**

Gomer Pyle, back of box.

Great Wild West, Universal, 1959, **$625.**

Great Wild West Bottle, Universal, 1959, **$225.**

Did you know...

*The Green Hornet survived as a minor character for a good half-century and has his share of adherents. At **$875** for this 1967 box from the TV show, collectors are among them. Did you know that The Green Hornet is a blood relative of The Lone Ranger? He is the Ranger's grand-nephew. They were created by the same man, Fran Striker.*

Green Hornet, King Seeley Thermos, 1967, **$875.**

Green Hornet Bottle, King Seeley Thermos, **$225.**

Grizzly Adams, The Life and Times of,
Aladdin, 1977, **$250.**

Grizzly Adams Bottle, The Life and Times of,
Aladdin, 1977, **$40.**

Guns of Will Sonnett, The, King Seeley Thermos, 1968, **$300.**

Guns of Will Sonnett Bottle, The, King Seeley Thermos,
1968, **$90.**

Gunsmoke, this version has the correct spelling of "Marshal," Aladdin, 1959, **$375.**

Did you know...

In 1959, Aladdin produced two versions of the
Gunsmoke lunch box, after the longest running
TV show of all time. This version, however, is the
important one. Instead of "U.S. Marshal," the box
says "U.S. Marshall." Aladdin quickly corrected the
mistake.

Gunsmoke, error box – the word Marshal is misspelled as
"Marshall," Aladdin, 1959, **$1,350.**

Gunsmoke Bottle, found at a yard sale in upstate
New York, Aladdin, 1959, **$95.**

Gunsmoke, Aladdin, 1962, **$450.**

Gunsmoke Bottle, Aladdin, 1962, **$95.**

Gunsmoke, Aladdin, 1972, **$275.**

Gunsmoke, back of box.

Gunsmoke Bottle, Aladdin, 1972, **$75.**

Gunsmoke, while the front scene is the same as the 1972 box, the back shown here was changed for 1973, Aladdin, 1973, **$350.**

Gunsmoke Bottle, Aladdin, 1973, **$75.**

Did you know...

*A very popular and sought-after lunch box, H.R.
Pufnstuf continues to intrigue today as much as it
did when the TV show ran on the BBC in the late
1960s for a season and for three seasons on NBC
in the states. The characters, the colors, the lingo ...
it all says 1970 so perfectly.*

H.R. Pufnstuf, Aladdin, 1970, **$850.**

H.R. Pufnstuf Bottle, Aladdin, 1970, **$110.**

Did you know...

Mid-to-late 1970s TV was dominated by Happy Days and its spin-offs (Laverne & Shirley, Mork & Mindy). Still pretty well available, this 1977 lunch box is still reachable as a beginning and intermediate collectible, and could come in handy in trading situations.

Happy Days, King Seeley Thermos, 1977, **$300.**

Happy Days Bottle, also used for The Fonz box, King Seeley Thermos, 1977-78, **$40.**

Happy Days, back of box.

Did you know...

Hector Heathcote, The Minute and a Half Man first debuted in 1959. He was a modern-day scientist that used a time machine to transport back to the days of the Revolutionary War and helped the American forces through all sorts of famous situations.

Hector Heathcote, Aladdin, 1964, **$325.**

Hector Heathcote Bottle, Aladdin, 1964, **$90.**

Did you know...

Unless there's a Johnny Cash lunch box somewhere out there that no one knows about, it's a good bet that the Hee Haw lunch box is the only one with two country music stars on it: Buck Owens (left) and Roy Clark. The show may have been cheesy, but the music was pure classic country.

Hee Haw, King Seeley Thermos, 1971, **$300.**

Hee Haw Bottle, King Seeley Thermos, 1971, **$75.**

Hogan's Heroes, Aladdin, 1966, **$725.**

Hogan's Heroes Bottle, Aladdin, 1966, **$200.**

Hogan's Heroes, back of box.

Did you know...

*Another lunch box that's priced like art, and
deservingly so, Home Town Airport perfectly
reflects America's obsession with flying in 1960.
The artwork on the box is sharp and stylish,
creating an enduring piece of American industrial
folk art.*

Home Town Airport, King Seeley Thermos, 1960, **$1,200.**

Home Town Airport Bottle, King Seeley Thermos, 1960, **$275.**

Did you know...

At **$550,** *mint Hopalong Cassidy lunch boxes are notable for their price as well as for being the first from the original era of kids' lunch boxes, 1954, to have the artwork done as full lithographs.*

Hopalong Cassidy, Aladdin, 1950,
the very first pictured box, **$550.**

Hopalong Cassidy Bottle, Aladdin, 1950, **$120.**

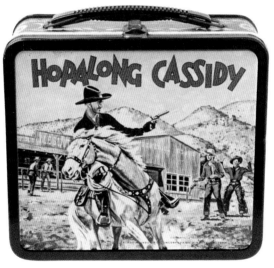

Hopalong Cassidy, this is the first full litho lunch box, Aladdin, 1954, **$850.**

Hopalong Cassidy Bottle, Aladdin, 1954, **$225.**

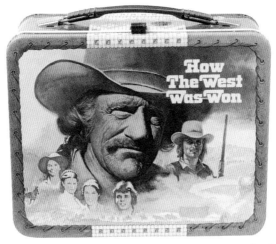

How The West Was Won, King Seeley Thermos, 1979, **$125.**

How The West Was Won Bottle,
King Seeley Thermos, 1979, **$40.**

Did you know...

One of the all-time great American children's shows, and one of the nation's first marketing juggernauts, Howdy Doody set the standard for decades to come. The lunch box was a huge part of that, so good examples bring good money.

Howdy Doody, Adco, 1954, **$1,100.**

Howdy Doody Bottle, this "generic" bottle was used in five different Adco boxes, 1954, **$250.**

Huckleberry Hound and His Friends, Aladdin, 1961, **$350.**

Huckleberry Hound and His Friends Bottle,
Aladdin, 1961, **$90.**

Indiana Jones and the Temple of Doom,
King Seeley Thermos, 1984, **$150.**

Indiana Jones and the Temple of Doom Bottle, used for both box versions, King Seeley Thermos, 1984, **$30.**

Indiana Jones and the Temple of Doom, second version, King Seeley Thermos, 1984, **$150.**

It's About Time, Aladdin, 1967, **$650.**

It's About Time Bottle, Aladdin, 1967, **$125.**

Jack and Jill, Ohio Arts, 1982, **$400.**

James Bond, Aladdin, 1966, **$775.**

James Bond Bottle, Aladdin, 1966, **$150.**

Did you know...

The ultimate super spy deserves the ultimate lunch box, right? Well, maybe it isn't the ultimate box, but it is a good one, set between Thunderball and You Only Live Twice. It's good to see Bond was keeping busy between big screen adventures.

James Bond XX, Ohio Arts, 1969, **$300.**

Jet Patrol, Aladdin, 1957, **$400.**

Jet Patrol Bottle, Aladdin, 1957, **$150.**

Did you know...

The 1963 Jetsons lunch box is a hugely important high-profile character box. The longstanding popularity of the original cartoon series, only 24 episodes in all, leads to high prices for the few remaining boxes that survive from the original marketing run of the series over the course of only six months, from 1962-'63.

Jetsons, front of box, Aladdin, 1963, **$2,650.**

Jetsons, back of box.

Jetsons Bottle, Aladdin, 1963, **$450.**

Jetsons, bottom of box.

Johnny Lightning, Aladdin, 1970, **$250.**

Johnny Lightning Bottle, Aladdin, 1970, **$60.**

Jonathan Livingston Seagull, Aladdin, 1973, **$150.**

Jonathan Livingston Seagull Bottle, Aladdin, 1973, **$50.**

Did you know...

A piece of marketing from the 1977 remake of the classic, what makes this King Kong lunch box so intriguing, and relatively expensive for the period, is the fact that the big ape is standing atop the twin towers.

King Kong, King Seeley Thermos, 1977, **$250.**

King Kong Bottle, King Seeley Thermos, 1977, **$40.**

KISS, King Seeley Thermos, 1977, **$400.**

KISS, back of box.

KISS Bottle, King Seeley Thermos, 1977, **$50.**

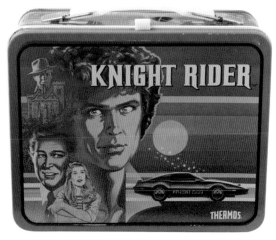

Knight Rider, King Seeley Thermos, 1984, **$95.**

Knight Rider Bottle, King Seeley Thermos, 1984, **$25.**

Knights in Armor, Universal, 1959, **$1,250.**

Did you know...

In the late 1950s, after a slew of Hollywood tales of knights and chivalry, along with the popularity of comic page hero Prince Valiant, Universal wisely cashed in on the craze among boys. Without a major character, box and bottle together can still bring about $1,600.

Knights in Armor, back of box.

Knights in Armor Bottle, Universal, 1957, **$300.**

Did you know...

Featuring Wonderbug on the front, The Krofft Supershow lunch box decided to go with the talking dune buggy as its lead character, trying to capitalize on the 1970s popularity of the Herbie The Love Bug movies. While he had a metallic bumper for lips and headlights for eyes, Wonderbug didn't last too long beyond his show.

Krofft Supershow, The, Aladdin, 1976, **$300.**

Krofft Supershow, The, Bottle, Aladdin, 1976, **$50.**

Kung Fu, King Seeley Thermos, 1974, **$250.**

Kung Fu Bottle, King Seeley Thermos, 1974, **$40.**

Land of the Lost, Aladdin, 1975, **$350.**

Land of the Lost Bottle, Aladdin, 1975, **$50.**

Did you know...

Laugh-In was the quintessential comedy of the late-1960s and early '70s. It was a must-stop for famous actors, comedians and even politicians of the day, most notably Richard Nixon.

Laugh-In, the Nazi Helmet version, Aladdin, 1968, **$325.**

Laugh-In Bottle, used with both box versions,
Aladdin, 1968, **$65.**

Laugh-In, the Tricycle version, Aladdin, 1971, **$375.**

Lawman, King Seeley Thermos, 1961, **$300.**

Lawman Bottle, King Seeley Thermos, 1961, **$85.**

Legend of the Lone Ranger, Aladdin, 1980, **$175.**

Legend of the Lone Ranger Bottle, Aladdin, 1980, **$45.**

Lidsville, Aladdin, 1971, **$375.**

Lidsville Bottle, Aladdin, 1971, **$65.**

Little Dutch Miss, Universal, 1959, **$225.**

Little Dutch Miss Bottle, Universal, 1959, **$75.**

Little Friends, Aladdin, 1982, **$850.**

Little Friends Bottle, Aladdin, 1982, **$260.**

Did you know...

Lunch boxes from the late 1970s and early '80s rarely achieve super high prices. At $350 for the best examples, Little House on the Prairie, after the popular TV show, is a bright spot in the age when overproduction reduced the potential collectibility of some good boxes.

Little House on the Prairie, King Seeley Thermos, 1978, **$350.**

Little House on the Prairie Bottle,
King Seeley Thermos, 1978, **$45.**

Did you know...

One of the best lunch boxes from the golden age of lunch box production—1954—The Lone Ranger lunch box is one of the most cherished memories for a couple generations of people, and a highly coveted high-profile character box.

Lone Ranger, Adco Liberty, 1954, **$1,150.**

Looney Tunes, used the same bottle as Porky's Lunch
Wagon, American Thermos, 1959, **$475.**

Did you know...

From 1965 to 1968, in 83 episodes, Lost in Space ruled the airwaves. Man had walked on the moon, manmade spacecraft were exploring our own galaxy and it seemed that in no time—by 1997, according to the show—humans would be able to do exactly what the Robinsons did, explore the universe with a talking robot in tow.

Lost in Space, King Seeley Thermos, 1967, **$1,350.**

Lost in Space Bottle, King Seeley Thermos, 1967, **$100.**

Ludwig Von Drake in Disneyland, Aladdin, 1962, **$475.**

Ludwig Von Drake in Disneyland Bottle, Aladdin, 1962, **$120.**

Man From U.N.C.L.E., The,
King Seeley Thermos, 1966, **$850.**

Man From U.N.C.L.E., The, Bottle,
King Seeley Thermos, 1966, **$100.**

Did you know...

While not particularly notable in terms of price, or art work, this lunch box is notable because it is one of the few entries in this book, and in the realm of classic lunch boxes, to feature classic Marvel characters. It came out in the mid-1970s when Marvel was undergoing a definite identity crisis in terms of the direction of its characters.

Marvel Comics' Super Heroes, Aladdin, 1976, **$200.**

Marvel Comics' Super Heroes Bottle, Aladdin, 1976, **$45.**

Mary Poppins, Aladdin, 1965, **$250.**

Mary Poppins Bottle, Aladdin, 1965, **$75.**

Mickey Mouse, front of box, Adco, 1954, **$1,000.**

Mickey Mouse, back of box.

Did you know...

This 1954 Mickey Mouse bottle brings almost double the price of what the original lunch box from which it came demands. It may be the same artwork, but it's a much rarer item to find, and much more expensive.

Mickey Mouse Bottle, Adco, 1954, **$1,850.**

Mickey Mouse Club, Aladdin, 1963, **$375.**

Mickey Mouse Club Bottle, Aladdin, 1963, **$60.**

Mickey Mouse Club, Aladdin, 1976, **$450.**

Mickey Mouse Club Bottle, Aladdin, 1976, **$90.**

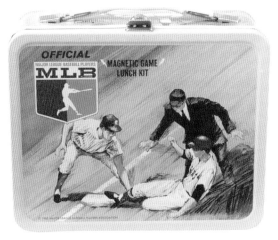

MLB, with game pieces, King Seeley Thermos, 1968, **$275.**

MLB Bottle, King Seeley Thermos, 1968, **$55.**

Monroes, The, Aladdin, 1967, **$550.**

Monroes Bottle, The, Aladdin, 1967, **$110.**

Mork & Mindy, King Seeley Thermos, 1979, **$175.**

Mork & Mindy Bottle, King Seeley Thermos, 1979, **$45.**

Did you know...

Still a popular franchise and TV show, The Munsters is one of the most popular high-profile character lunch boxes. The whole family is on both the front and back, looking every bit as suburban and domesticated as any of their neighbors. For 70 episodes, The Munsters was the blue-collar answer to The Addams Family.

Munsters, The, King Seeley Thermos, 1966, **$900.**

Munsters, The, back of box.

Munsters, The, Bottle, King Seeley Thermos, 1966, **$150.**

Muppet Babies, King Seeley Thermos, 1985, **$75.**

Muppet Babies Bottle, King Seeley Thermos, 1985, **$20.**

Did you know...

*Jim Henson's lovable Muppets were never more popular than in 1979, when the TV show was number one with kids and adults alike, and The Muppet Movie was gangbusters in American box offices. At **$225,** the price is good for a production from the era of overproduction.*

Muppet Movie, King Seeley Thermos, 1979, **$225.**

Muppet Movie Bottle, King Seeley Thermos, 1979, **$40.**

Muppet Show, King Seeley Thermos, 1978, **$150.**

Muppet Show Bottle, King Seeley Thermos, 1978, **$30.**

Muppets, King Seeley Thermos, 1979, **$125.**

Muppets, back of box featured Fozzie, Animal, or Kermit.

Muppets Bottle, King Seeley Thermos, 1979, **$30.**

Did you know...

Like so many of the organized national sport league boxes from the 1960s, this NFL box doesn't feature a single marquee team, but does at least feature the 13 teams in the AFL on the front, and one would suppose the 13 NFL teams on the back. The bottle however, has them all.

NFL, Universal, 1962, **$350.**

NFL Bottle, Universal, 1962, **$130.**

NHL, Okay Industries, 1970, **$600.**

NHL Bottle, also used for Boston Bruins box,
Okay Industries, **$250.**

Orbit a.k.a. John Glenn, NASA made KST remove this box from market because the depiction was too accurate, very rare, King Seeley Thermos, 1963, **$500.**

Partridge Family, The, Bottle, first version,
King Seeley Thermos, 1971, **$60.**

Partridge Family, The, Bottle, second version,
King Seeley Thermos, 1971, **$60.**

Partridge Family, The, King Seeley Thermos, 1971, **$275.**

Pathfinder, Universal, 1959, **$750.**

Pathfinder Bottle, w/compass – maybe 2 percent of the boxes came with these very rare accessories, Universal, 1959, **$225.**

Did you know...

*The 1960s Peanuts dome boxes, particularly the Snoopy box, are worth less than the standard 1966 King Seeley boxes, but at **$325**, this box is still affordable and still plenty desirable. Charlie Brown, Snoopy, Linus, Lucy and Schroeder, the core of the gang, hang out and listen to Schroeder jam.*

Peanuts, King Seeley Thermos, 1966, **$325**.

Peanuts Bottle, the same used for both versions of the
Snoopy Dome box, King Seeley Thermos, 1966, **$50.**

Peanuts, King Seeley Thermos, 1980, **$125.**

Peanuts Bottle, King Seeley Thermos, 1980, **$35.**

Did you know...

Let's face it, the early 1960s teenage Pebbles &
Bamm-Bamm cartoon show was a little creepy,
a little forced and a little too progressive for its
time. At **$300** it's still a good piece to have in a
collection, but to fans of The Flintstones, it was off
the mark.

Pebbles & Bamm-Bamm, Aladdin, 1961, **$300.**

Pebbles & Bamm-Bamm Bottle, Aladdin, 1961, **$60.**

Pelé, King Seeley Thermos, 1975, **$250.**

Pelé Bottle, King Seeley Thermos, 1975, **$45.**

Pete's Dragon, Aladdin, 1978, **$150.**

Pete's Dragon Bottle, Aladdin, 1978, **$35.**

Peter Pan, Aladdin, 1969, **$325.**

Peter Pan Bottle, Aladdin, 1969, **$50.**

Pigs in Space, King Seeley Thermos, 1977, **$75.**

Pigs in Space Bottle, King Seeley Thermos, 1977, **$30**.

Pinocchio, Aladdin, 1971, **$350.**

Pinocchio Bottle, Aladdin, 1971, **$50.**

Did you know...

From the short-lived 1974 TV series, The Planet of the Apes lunch box encompasses the entire plot of the 14-episode show: bad gorillas, good chimps, wise baboons and well-coiffed humans. The series did somehow manage to get Roddy McDowell to don his ape suit one more time.

Planet of the Apes, Aladdin, 1974, **$525.**

Planet of the Apes, back of box.

Planet of the Apes Bottle, Aladdin, 1974, **$95.**

Police Patrol, Aladdin, 1978, **$300.**

Police Patrol Bottle, Aladdin, 1978, **$45.**

Did you know...

Few characters have lasted as long in American culture as Popeye. There is, in fact, an entire level of the toy collecting hobby dedicated just to the squinty-eyed sailor with the giant forearms and anchor tattoos. Lunch box collectors compete with those collectors for a prize such as this.

Popeye, Universal, 1962, **$900.**

Popeye Bottle, Universal, 1962, **$600.**

Popeye, King Seeley Thermos, 1964, **$450.**

Popeye Bottle, King Seeley Thermos, 1964, **$80.**

Popeye, Aladdin, 1980, **$200**.

Popeye Bottle, Aladdin, 1980, **$45.**

Did you know...

This dome-top box from the late-1950s features virtually the entire Loony Tunes cast and is another example of why the dome-top boxes remain so popular: good art, good quality, great subject. On the back, Bugs is stealing Porky's business with a Wagon of his own.

Porky's Lunch Wagon, American Thermos, 1959, **$625.**

Porky's Lunch Wagon, bottom of box.

Porky's Lunch Wagon Bottle, American Thermos, 1959, **$125.**

Quarterback, Aladdin, 1964, **$375.**

Quarterback Bottle, Aladdin, 1964, **$90.**

Racing Wheels, King Seeley Thermos, 1977, **$150.**

Racing Wheels Bottle, King Seeley Thermos, 1977, **$25.**

Rambo, last metal box the company produced, King
Seeley Thermos, 1985, **$95.**

Rambo Bottle, King Seeley Thermos, 1985, **$20.**

Rat Patrol, Aladdin, 1967, **$400.**

Rat Patrol Bottle, Aladdin, 1967, **$90.**

Rifleman, The, Aladdin, 1961, **$675.**

Rifleman, The, Bottle, Aladdin, 1961, **$175.**

Road Runner, The, King Seeley Thermos, 1970, **$275.**

Road Runner, The, Bottle, King Seeley Thermos,
1970, **$75.**

Robin Hood, Aladdin, 1956, **$550.**

Robin Hood Bottle, Aladdin, 1956, **$150.**

Did you know...

Who knows what the McDonald's Corp. was thinking with this lunch box in 1982. It was the age of overproduction, and an era of transition for the signature characters of the fast food giant, so maybe they figured out that a little frontier justice would set things straight.

Ronald McDonald Sheriff of Cactus Canyon, Aladdin, 1982, **$125.**

Ronald McDonald Sheriff of Cactus Canyon Bottle,
Aladdin, 1982, **$20.**

Rough Rider, Aladdin, 1973, **$125.**

Rough Rider Bottle, first version, Aladdin, 1973, **$40.**

Rough Rider Bottle, second version, Aladdin, **$40.**

Roy Rogers, this is the first Roy Rogers box,
American Thermos, 1953, **$350.**

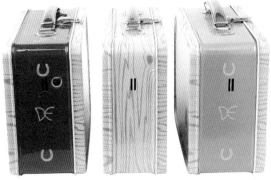

Roy Rogers. Different sidebands were used: red, 1954; woodgrain, 1953; blue, 1954.

Roy Rogers Bottle, American Thermos, 1953, **$90.**

Roy Rogers, w/leather handle, Canada only, American Thermos, 1954, **$350.**

Roy Rogers, rearing Trigger, American Thermos, 1955, **$375.**

Roy Rogers Double R Bar Ranch,
American Thermos, 1955, **$350.**

Roy Rogers, 8-scenes box, American Thermos, 1955, **$375.**

Roy Rogers Chow Wagon Dome, King Seeley Thermos,
1958, **$525.**

Roy Rogers Chow Wagon Bottle,
King Seeley Thermos, 1958, **$95.**

Roy Rogers, a.k.a. Red Shirt or On The Rail, American Thermos, 1958, **$450.**

Roy Rogers Bottle, this was used for both the Chow Wagon and the Red Shirt boxes, American Thermos, **$95.**

Saddlebag, King Seeley Thermos, 1977, **$195.**

Saddlebag Bottle, King Seeley Thermos, 1977, **$40.**

Satellite, King Seeley Thermos, 1960, **$350.**

School Days, Mickey Mouse in the classroom,
Aladdin, 1984, **$600.**

School Days Bottle, Aladdin, 1984, **$175.**

Did you know...

*The two Scooby Doo lunch boxes from King Seeley bring **$750 and $800** (yellow & orange rim) and feature Scooby and Shaggy, the cartoon's most popular characters, running from the Headless Horseman, the villain from the show's most popular episode.*

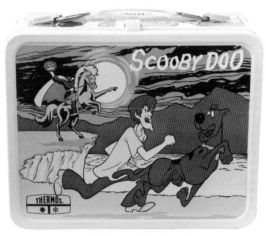

Scooby Doo, yellow border,
King Seeley Thermos, 1973, **$750.**

Scooby Doo Bottle, goes with yellow rim box,
King Seeley Thermos, 1973, **$50.**

Scooby Doo, orange rim,
King Seeley Thermos, 1973, **$800.**

Scooby Doo Bottle, goes with orange rim box,
King Seeley Thermos, 1973, **$50.**

Secret Agent, King Seeley Thermos, 1968, **$325.**

Secret Agent Bottle, King Seeley Thermos, 1968, **$75.**

Sesame Street, Aladdin, 1983, **$125.**

Sesame Street Bottle, Aladdin, 1983, **$30.**

Six Million Dollar Man, The,
King Seeley Thermos, 1974, **$200.**

Six Million Dollar Man, The, Bottle,
King Seeley Thermos, 1974, **$40.**

Six Million Dollar Man, The,
King Seeley Thermos, 1978, **$225.**

Six Million Dollar Man, The, Bottle,
King Seeley Thermos, 1978, **$40.**

Skateboarder, Aladdin, 1977, **$175.**

Skateboarder Bottle, Aladdin, 1977, **$40.**

Sleeping Beauty, General Steelwares, Canada, **$450.**

Did you know...

One of the original environmental icons, Smokey Bear taught children of the 1960s and '70s that only they "could prevent forest fires." The box and the bottle together are very desirable and can bring as much as **$900** together.

Smokey Bear, Okay Industries, 1975, **$550.**

Smokey Bear Bottle, rare, Okay Industries, 1975, **$350.**

Smurfs, King Seeley Thermos, 1983, **$225.**

Smurfs Bottle, King Seeley Thermos, 1983, **$30.**

Snoopy Dome, red cup in Snoopy's hand,
King Seeley Thermos, **$225.**

Snoopy Dome, blue cup in Snoopy's hand,
King Seeley Thermos, **$450.**

Space Shuttle, King Seeley Thermos, 1977, **$250.**

Space Shuttle Bottle, King Seeley Thermos, 1977, **$45.**

Space: 1999, King Seeley Thermos, 1976, **$300.**

Space: 1999 Bottle, King Seeley Thermos, 1976, **$40.**

Did you know...

In the late 1950s, baseball was still king in America. Ohio Arts—famously the makers of Etch-a-Sketch—produced this sports-themed box to try and appeal to boys who watched multiple sports and didn't have a particular team. You can only imagine that the audience for it wasn't too big. Nor is the price for it more than 50 years later.

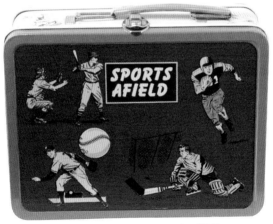

Sports Afield, Ohio Arts, 1957, **$275.**

Did you know...

In mint condition, the 1968 Star Trek lunch box is one of the rarest and most sought after of all boxes. The reasons for this are many, as few TV shows have so thoroughly and enduringly captured America's imagination. Along with the bottle, these two can bring almost $3,000.

Star Trek, front of box shows the U.S.S. Enterprise, Aladdin, 1968, **$2,350.**

Star Trek, back of box shows Mr. Spock and Captain Kirk.

Star Trek, bottom of box shows the bridge of the Enterprise.

Star Trek Bottle, Aladdin, 1968, **$450.**

Star Trek: The Motion Picture,
King Seeley Thermos, 1980, **$300.**

Star Trek: The Motion Picture Bottle,
King Seeley Thermos, 1980, **$60.**

Did you know...

You might think the Seeley Thermos lunch box from the first *Star Wars* movie would be worth a good deal more than **$300,** given the movie's impact on popular culture. Alas, George Lucas and Co. quickly figured out the secret of mass marketing, making these boxes still relatively easy to get a hold of.

Star Wars, King Seeley Thermos, 1978, **$300.**

Star Wars, two different sidebands were used on this box.

Star Wars Bottle, King Seeley Thermos, 1978, **$40.**

Star Wars: The Empire Strikes Back, ship scene, King
Seeley Thermos, 1980, **$250.**

Star Wars: The Empire Strikes Back Bottle,
King Seeley Thermos, 1980, **$30.**

Star Wars: The Empire Strikes Back, Dagobah scene, King
Seeley Thermos, 1981, **$250.**

Star Wars: The Empire Strikes Back Bottle, King Seeley
Thermos, 1981, **$40.**

Star Wars: Return of the Jedi,
King Seeley Thermos, 1983, **$150.**

Star Wars: Return of the Jedi Bottle,
King Seeley Thermos, 1983, **$30.**

Star Wars: Return of the Jedi Bottle,
King Seeley Thermos, 1983, **$30.**

Steve Canyon, Aladdin, 1959, **$575.**

Steve Canyon Bottle, Aladdin, 1959, **$150.**

Street Hawk, Aladdin, 1985, **$365.**

Street Hawk Bottle, Aladdin, 1985, **$90.**

Did you know...

The Super Friends and Super Powers lunch boxes, while valuable and available at the low end of the spectrum, are examples of titles that can be picked up for relatively little during tough economic times and kept for better days.

Super Friends, Aladdin, 1976, **$195.**

Super Friends Bottle, Aladdin, 1976, **$40.**

Super Powers, Aladdin, 1983, **$175.**

Super Powers Bottle, Aladdin, 1983, **$40.**

Supercar, Universal, 1962, **$475.**

Supercar Bottle, Universal, 1962, **$150.**

Did you know...

Quite simply put, the Adco 1954 Superman lunch box, in mint condition, is the Holy Grail of lunch box collecting. The price says it, the character says it, and every collector will say it. Pristine examples are very hard to come by, and rarely parted with when acquired. The Man of Steel always has been, and always will be, number one.

Superman, front of box, Adco, 1954, **$16,500.**

Superman, back of box.

Superman Bottle, this "generic" bottle was used in five
different Adco boxes, Adco, 1954, **$250.**

Did you know...

While some 13 years later than the 1954 original, King Seeley produced the Superman Bottle, which today can easily bring more than $1,200, given that the 1954 boxes came with generic red & yellow Thermoses.

Superman Bottle, King Seeley Thermos, 1967, **$1,200.**

Superman, King Seeley Thermos, 1967, **$125.**

Superman, Aladdin, 1978, **$250.**

Superman Bottle, Aladdin, 1978, **$50.**

Tarzan, Aladdin, 1966, **$475.**

Tarzan Bottle, Aladdin, 1966, **$75.**

Tom Corbett Space Cadet, blue box, Aladdin, 1952, **$450.**

Tom Corbett Space Cadet, red box, Aladdin, 1952, **$450.**

Tom Corbett Space Cadet Bottle, either the red top or yellow top bottle came with the blue 1952 box, **$95.**

Tom Corbett Space Cadet Bottle,
the red top bottle came with the red 1952 box, **$95.**

This is the 1954 Tom Corbett full litho lunch box with yellow cup bottle. **$850** for box, **$125** for the bottle.

Toppie Elephant, American Thermos,
1957; **$3,850** box, **$800** bottle.
From the Julie Rose Collection

Did you know...

While the Track King lunch box is a valuable mid-range box, the Track King bottle is one of the rarest bottle's in the entire collecting hobby. With only three examples known, if you see one at a garage sale grab it and run.

Track King, Okay Industries, 1975, **$350.**

Track King Bottle, Okay Industries, 1975, **$650.**

Treasure Chest, Aladdin, 1961, **$375.**

Treasure Chest Bottle, Aladdin, 1961, **$90.**

Trigger, American Thermos, 1956, **$700.**

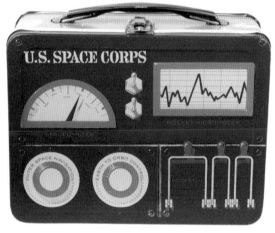

U.S. Space Corps, Universal, 1961, **$525.**

U.S. Space Corps Bottle, Universal, 1961, **$150.**

Did you know...

Originally conceived of to sell breakfast cereal via cartoons, Underdog spent his days as the humble "Shoeshine Boy" and his nights as Underdog, fighting criminals and saving his love, Polly. The price reflects the rarity, desirability and popularity of the character. The bottle, by itself, is worth **$1,250,** *making the pair, in mint condition, worth almost* **$5,000.**

Underdog, Okay Industries, 1974, **$3,500.**

Underdog Bottle, Okay Industries, 1974, **$1,250.**

Universal Movie Monsters, Aladdin, 1979, **$400.**

Universal Movie Monsters, back of box.

Universal Movie Monsters Bottle, Aladdin, 1979, **$50.**

V, Aladdin, 1984, **$300.**

V Bottle, Aladdin, 1984, **$75.**

Voyage to the Bottom of the Sea, Aladdin, 1967, **$750**.

Voyage to the Bottom of the Sea Bottle,
Aladdin, 1967, **$175.**

Did you know...

Given away as a premium from participating VW dealerships in the 1960s, the VW bus lunch box will still bring high three figure prices among collectors of both lunch boxes and Volkswagon and car memorabilia.

VW Bus, premium at Volkswagen dealerships, Omni Graphics, 1960s, **$850.**

VW Bus, view of the open box.

VW Bus Bottle, two versions of the bottle,
Omni Graphics, 1960s, **$275.**

Wake Up America, Okay Industries, 1973, **$700.**

Wake Up America Bottle, Okay Industries, 1973, **$250**.

Walt Disney's Wonderful World, back of box,
Aladdin, 1982, **$125.**

Walt Disney's Wonderful World Bottle, Aladdin, 1982, **$30.**

Waltons, The, Aladdin, 1973, **$325.**

Waltons, The, Bottle, Aladdin, 1973, **$40.**

Washington Redskins, Okay Industries, 1970, **$375.**

Washington Redskins Bottle, Okay Industries, 1970, **$140.**

Did you know...

It was 1977 and America was getting its first taste of Welcome Back, Kotter and a young actor named John Travolta. While the box itself is a well-priced lower end character box, it's notable for its era and for its depiction of Travolta before he became a massive star.

Welcome Back, Kotter, Aladdin, 1977, **$275.**

Welcome Back, Kotter Bottle, Aladdin, 1977, **$50.**

Westerner, King Seeley Thermos, 1963, **$275.**

Westerner, back of box.

Wild Wild West, The, Aladdin, 1969, **$700.**

Wild Wild West, The, Bottle, Aladdin, 1969, **$120.**

Winnie the Pooh, Aladdin, 1967, **$325.**

Winnie the Pooh Bottle, Aladdin, 1967, **$80.**

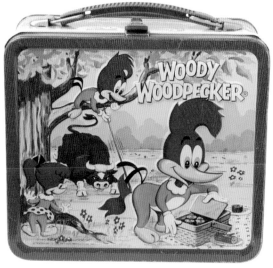

Woody Woodpecker, Aladdin, 1972, **$450.**

Woody Woodpecker Bottle, Aladdin, 1972, **$90.**

Did you know...

One of the most popular lunch boxes, period, and one of the most popular Beatles collectibles, period, do you want to own this beautiful piece of pop culture, with The Nowhere Man, The Blue Meanies and the boys from Liverpool? You'll have plenty of competition.

Yellow Submarine, King Seeley Thermos, 1968, **$1,300.**

Yellow Submarine, back of box.

Yellow Submarine Bottle, King Seeley Thermos, 1968, **$350.**

Did you know...

At $350, this box is still affordable but a little bit up market for some collectors. If the box was just Yogi, or Yogi and Boo-Boo, one can imagine that the price would go up significantly, nothing against the mice, Pixie and Dixie, and the cat, Mr. Jinks.

Yogi Bear and Friends, Aladdin, 1961, **$350.**

Yogi Bear and Friends Bottle, Aladdin, 1961, **$80.**

Yogi Bear, Aladdin, 1974, **$325.**

Yogi Bear Bottle, Aladdin, 1974, **$60.**

Zorro, front of box, Aladdin, 1966, **$650.**

Zorro, back of box.